S0-AAB-588

RUTH

Woman of Loyalty

Kjersti Hoff Baez

Illustrated by
Al Bohl

BARBOUR
PUBLISHING

© 1990 by Barbour Publishing, Inc.

ISBN 1-58660-942-4

All rights reserved. No part of this publication may be reproduced or transmitted in any form or by any means without written permission of the publisher.

Published by Barbour Publishing, Inc., P.O. Box 719, Uhrichsville, Ohio 44683, www.barbourbooks.com

Member of the
Evangelical Christian
Publishers Association

Printed in the United States of America.
5 4 3 2 1

RUTH

"RUTH, LET ME TAKE THE BABY."

1

LAND OF SORROW

The young woman cuddled the sleeping baby close to her heart. She stood at the edge of a meadow and sighed happily at the poppies blooming there. Bright reds and yellows swayed in the breeze in a blaze of color.

"Ruth!" someone called to the woman. "Let me take the baby. He should be inside sleeping, not outside like some miserable nomad." Naomi scooped the baby from Ruth's arms and smiled. "Besides, look at the sky! It's bound to rain."

The young woman glanced up at the sky and watched as clouds stumbled over one another in preparation for a storm. Naomi hurried into the house, but Ruth stayed behind. The breeze grew stronger, and the wild flowers bowed before the coming storm. As she lingered under the darkening sky, the storm's first raindrops tickled her face, and, with their touch, Ruth remembered another day, another storm, and another place. . . .

Ruth lifted her face to the stormy sky and let the rain mingle with her tears. She felt lost and her heart pounded with the realization that she would never see her young husband again. Mahlon was dead.

"Let's go home, Ruth." Naomi's voice was weary with grief as she turned to leave the tomb. A small cluster of women dressed in black followed after Naomi like a dark cloud. Their cries of mourning filled the air with sorrow.

Ruth stood for a moment, staring at the cave

"TRY TO BE STILL."

where her husband's body had been laid. "Home," she said to herself. The word that had once brought such happiness to Ruth now stabbed her with pain. She followed Naomi up the path and down the road to their house. The storm clouds darkened as if in sympathy with the young widow, and the rain fell more fiercely on the rolling hills of Moab.

Ruth's sister-in-law, Orpah, met Naomi and Ruth at the door of their home. Her face was veiled in black and her eyes were dark with worry.

"It's Chilion. His fever is worse." Her voice trembled with fear. "It's just like Mahlon. He doesn't recognize me and—"

Naomi swept past her daughter-in-law and hurried to the corner of the room where Chilion lay on his mat. He tossed back and forth on the mat, groaning with pain. Naomi knelt beside him and grasped his hand.

"Chilion," she said desperately. "Try and be still. Everything is going to be all right."

Naomi's son looked up at her for a moment. He

stared at her and trembled with fever. She searched her son's face for a flicker of recognition, but none came. He did not know who she was. Naomi rose to her feet with a sigh.

"He will be dead by tomorrow," she said quietly. "The Almighty has turned His hand against me." She tore at her mourning clothes. "I will wear sackcloth for the rest of my life."

The next day Chilion died. The men of the village came and buried him in his brother's tomb. Naomi's neighbors surrounded the three grieving women and shook their heads in dismay.

"Surely the gods are angry with you," crackled the voice of an old woman known as the Old One. "Perhaps you had better sacrifice to the mighty Chemosh, Naomi."

"Keep your gods to yourself," spat Naomi. "It is the Almighty who has forsaken me."

"Well, I don't see what good your god has done for you," retorted the woman, her face puckered with wrinkles. "After all, first your husband, and

"THE GODS ARE ANGRY WITH YOU."

now both your sons are dead. So much for the power of Yahweh."

Naomi trembled with anger, but Ruth and Orpah gently pulled her away from the crowd. Together they trudged back to the house. Orpah pulled open the wooden door and followed Naomi inside. An oil lamp glimmered from its ledge in the wall, casting eerie shadows in the darkened room. Ruth stood frozen in the doorway, overwhelmed by the emptiness that glared out at her from the room that had been her home.

Ruth ran from the house and stumbled to the edge of a ridge, where she looked out at the highlands of Moab. The sun was making its faithful journey downward, leaving behind traces of splendor in red and orange. A mist hung over the mountains and Ruth gazed westward. Behind those hills lay Mahlon's homeland. As the sunset shimmered over Ruth's tears, she wondered if the glow of color would ever return to her life. She pulled her black sackcloth tighter and shivered in the coolness of the evening.

There had to be something more to life than sackcloth and sorrow. Ruth searched the horizon as if looking for a refuge, a place to hide. Something tugged at her heart, and for a moment she thought she heard someone call her name. Startled, she looked around but only caught a glimpse of an eagle as it flashed by on the way to its nest in the mountains.

Several weeks later, Naomi called her two daughters-in-law together and outlined her plan for them.

"Laban the merchant tells me the famine in Judah is over and that the Almighty has blessed his people with food. Our only hope is to journey to my home in Bethlehem. Perhaps we will be able to survive there."

"When do we leave?" asked Orpah.

"In three days, Laban and some others are traveling to Judah. We will journey with them."

Naomi looked sadly at Ruth and Orpah. "I know it will be difficult for you to leave your homeland here. But what other choice do we have? No,

"PERHAPS I SHOULD NEVER HAVE LEFT JUDAH."

my dear ones, we must leave this land of death. Go and say good-bye to your mothers."

She watched as Ruth and Orpah walked through the door into the afternoon sunlight and closed the door behind them. The ever-present oil lamp sputtered at her from its place in the wall.

"Perhaps," she muttered to herself, "I should never have left Judah in the first place."

2

SAYING GOOD-BYE

"You are a fool!" Ruth's mother hovered around her like an angry bird of prey. "You can't leave Moab with that woman. She's a Hebrew! You will be miserable."

"She is my husband's mother."

"Your husband is dead."

Ruth said nothing, but the tears in her eyes spoke for her. Her mother's tone softened.

"Listen," she whispered. Her eyes darted furtively around the room as if there might be someone

A SACRIFICE FOR CHEMOSH

listening. "Perhaps the Old One is right. Perhaps you have angered Chemosh." Stepping back to the corner of the room, she picked up a small wooden cage and placed it in Ruth's hands.

"This is for you," she said. "Take it to the high place outside the village near the old almond tree. Offer it to Chemosh and beg for mercy."

Ruth looked into the cage at the small brown pigeon that cowered inside.

"It won't hurt to beg Baal, either." The fear and bondage in her mother's voice penetrated Ruth's heart with icy fingers. She felt her mother's arms around her and heard her whisper in her ear. "Go now. Offer it to the gods. Hurry."

Ruth hurried out the door and fairly flew to the high place. Several worshipers were there ahead of Ruth, and the pile of stones that served as an altar sizzled with blood and fire as they offered their sacrifices to the mighty Chemosh. The familiar chanting and wailing filled Ruth's ears and she shuddered. The chanting grew louder, and the worshipers motioned

RELEASING THE SACRIFICE

to Ruth to join them and make an offering. Suddenly, someone screamed. It was the Old One.

"Come!" she screamed at Ruth. "Come to the altar!"

Ruth nearly passed out with fear. The next thing she knew, she was running from the high place, hugging the cage to her chest. She stopped at a small clearing at the edge of a barley field. She gently drew the trembling bird from the cage and held it for a moment in her hands. Then she lifted it up to the sky and set it free. The pigeon's wings fluttered swiftly in the afternoon air, and Ruth watched as it escaped, a soft brown blur against the bright blue sky.

"I wish I could join you, little bird," the young widow whispered, watching until the pigeon disappeared. Then she turned toward the village. Her sad eyes could not see the poppies blooming by the edge of the road, nor could she hear the laughter of a little boy running in the fields nearby.

Two days later, Naomi placed the last of their

baskets on the back of one of Laban's donkeys.

"That donkey is fortunate that we are poor!" she said, gazing at the few baskets loaded on the animal. "He has only a light burden to carry!" She smiled at her two daughters-in-law and sighed. "If only my burdens were so light!"

"Eeyaah!" Laban's hoarse voice bellowed. "We're off!" At his signal, the small group of people and donkeys started their journey.

"Does the man have to yell?" Naomi groaned under her breath. She motioned to Ruth and Orpah, and they fell into place behind the small group of travelers. "May the God of Israel at least grant us mercy on our way."

The early morning sun showered sparkle on the dew and Orpah gazed with longing at the fields that stretched out beside the road. Naomi watched her for a moment and then looked quickly away. Ruth looked straight ahead, her mind still numb with grief, and the screams of the Old One ringing in her ears.

They had not traveled far when Naomi stopped

LEAVING HOME

in the road and began to weep.

"I cannot do it," she cried. "I cannot do it."

Ruth and Orpah gathered around their mother-in-law and took her by the hand.

"What is the matter, Mother?" Orpah asked. "Why are you crying?"

Naomi shook her head. "It's no use," she sobbed. "I won't do this to you." She pointed back to their village. "Go back. Go back where you belong."

"What are you talking about, Mother?" Ruth's voice trembled.

"You must go back to the homes of your mothers. It would not be right for me to take you away from your homeland and your families. Go, my daughters. May the Lord be kind to you as you have been to me and to my sons."

She kissed them both and turned to leave them.

"No, Mother, no." The two young widows wept. "We'll go with you."

Naomi shook her head and looked sadly at their young faces.

ORPAH RETURNS TO THE VILLAGE.

"What do I have to offer you?" she asked. "Will I marry again and have two more sons for you to marry? And even if I did have two more sons, would you wait for them to grow up? No, my dears, you still have a chance for a good life here in your own country, with your own people. Go back. And may the Lord give you refuge in the home of another husband."

They wept all the more as Naomi begged them to return, and finally Orpah looked back at the village they had left behind. She kissed Naomi and Ruth good-bye, retrieved her basket from the donkey, and turned back toward the village. Naomi buried her face in her hands and sobbed.

"Surely the Almighty has set His hand against me," Naomi cried. "He has left me all alone." She looked up, fully expecting to be alone, but to her surprise Ruth stood still beside her in the road.

"What are you doing, Ruth?" she asked. She pointed to Orpah's figure hurrying toward the village. "See, Orpah is going back to her people and her gods. Why don't you go with her?"

"WHEREVER YOU GO, I WILL GO."

Ruth clung to her mother-in-law. "Please don't tell me to leave you. Wherever you go, I will go, and where you stay, I will stay, too. Your people will be my people, and your God will be my own. Where you die, so will I, and there I will be laid to rest. May the Lord deal harshly with me if anything but death separates me from you."

Ruth's words touched Naomi's bitter heart, and a faint whisper of hope stirred within her. There was a stubborn look in Ruth's eyes; wordlessly, Naomi took her by the arm. Together they hurried to catch up with their fellow travelers.

3

A Troublesome Start

"So, have you made up your minds?" Laban shouted to Ruth and Naomi as they caught up with the caravan. "You've got to keep up or we'll leave you in the dust!"

Naomi glared at the merchant. "We can keep up. Just mind your own business."

Laban marched back to the two women, his eyes flashing.

"This is my business. I have never once lost a

"YOU'VE GOT TO KEEP UP!"

man or animal on the trail, and I don't intend to start losing anyone now." He jerked his oily face close to Ruth and Naomi. "You know," he said, "there are bandits and wild beasts all over the wilderness. If you straggle behind, no telling what might happen." He looked to see if the women shuddered with fear. Naomi gave him a blank look.

"Besides," he continued. "I have a reputation that precedes me from Edom to Judah."

Naomi glanced at his rather stout stomach.

"That's not all that precedes you," murmured Naomi.

"Don't say I didn't warn you," Laban shouted as he stomped back to the front of the caravan.

"Do you think we will make it safely to Judah?" Ruth asked Naomi with fear in her voice.

"Don't worry." Naomi patted Ruth on the hand. "We'll do fine. Don't listen to that loudmouth Laban. He's just trying to scare us. Besides," she said, sighing and adjusting the black veil around her head, "could anything worse happen to us?"

Ruth said nothing, and they walked on together in silence. The morning sky shone blue and glorious above the small band of pilgrims. The young widow breathed in the cool air and let her thoughts wander over the last few days. She thought of Mahlon and how he used to smile at her and laugh at her auburn hair.

"Where did you get that hair?" he used to say. "You're supposed to have black hair like everybody else. You must be an angel."

Ruth blushed at the memory, and tears sprang quickly to her eyes. She hid her tears from Naomi and fixed her eyes on the dusty road at her feet.

"I must be strong," she thought to herself. "I must be strong for Naomi." She looked over at her mother-in-law. Naomi trudged along, her face creased with despair.

Ruth straightened her shoulders and tried not to feel so small beneath the widening sky. She caught glimpses of the desert to the east of the plateau on which they traveled. Flocks of sheep draped the hills

THOUGHTS OF MAHLON

like wisps of cotton, and once in awhile the faint whisper of a shepherd's flute teased the air with a hint of music.

"Take a good look," the thought intruded on Ruth's mind. "You're leaving everything you've ever known. Your home, everything. Turn back now, while there's still time." But a black wisp of smoke rising eerily from one of the high places smeared the sky, and Ruth knew she would never go back.

The morning coolness disappeared quickly, and the afternoon sun warmed the faces of the travelers. Ruth was getting tired, and the glare of the sun threatened to put her to sleep. The monotony of their journey added to her weariness and she wondered when they were going to stop and rest. All at once, the donkeys stopped moving forward.

"What now?" Laban yelled. He pulled at the lead donkey with no success. "At the rate we're going, we'll never reach Dibon before nightfall."

"So what are we going to do?" someone asked from among the group. Everyone started talking at

"SOMETHING IS WRONG."

once until Laban raised his hand for silence.

"Something is wrong," he whispered. "I can feel it."

In the momentary silence, everyone froze in anticipation. Suddenly, something darted across the road in front of the donkeys. It was a small deer. Everyone sighed with relief.

"Your donkeys are afraid of that?" someone said, laughing.

Their laughter was cut short. With a bellowing roar, a huge lion tore across the road in a streak of fury. It paid no attention to the frightened caravan but relentlessly pursued the frightened deer.

Ruth watched as the hunter and hunted disappeared into a distant ravine. The lion's roar swelled again, and in the silence that followed Ruth knew the tiny deer had lost its race for life.

"That was close!" Laban said, wiping his brow with his sleeve. "Good thing that lion didn't change his menu in the middle of his meal!" He laughed and slapped the dust from his sandals.

A LION ROARED.

"Very funny," someone muttered.

"Oh, well," Laban continued. "A full lion is a happy lion. Let's get out of here. We'll be stopping at Dibon for the night. It won't be long now."

"Eeyaah!" Laban's voice echoed across the hills. "We're off!"

They reached Dibon just as the sun slipped behind the western hills. Laban directed Ruth and Naomi to the home of a fellow merchant.

"You'll have to sleep on the roof," Laban told them, "but that's better than sleeping on the ground, eh?"

The two women gratefully climbed the outer steps that led to the roof of the merchant's house.

"We'll be leaving first thing in the morning," Laban called up to them. "Be at the northern end of town by sunrise."

"Why don't you tell the whole neighborhood our business?" Naomi hissed at him from the top of the stairs.

"All right, all right," Laban lowered his voice. "Just

be there on time." He spat on the ground. "Miserable old camel," he muttered under his breath.

Stubborn mule, Naomi thought.

Naomi found two mats in a pile of baskets in the corner of the roof, and she gave one to Ruth.

They unrolled the mats and lay down under the stars.

From the top of the roof, Ruth looked out at the town of Dibon. The whitewashed houses were clustered together, and in the moonlight, they resembled a huddle of tired sheep. The excitement of being in a new place kept her awake.

"Tell me about your husband, Naomi," Ruth asked. "What was he like?"

Naomi sighed and closed her eyes. "Aren't you tired, daughter?"

"No, not really. What was Elimelech like?"

"He was a good man," Naomi said, "but he was a worrier. He was a good farmer, but when the famine came, he panicked. And so we left Bethlehem and came to Moab."

LOOKING AT THE TOWN OF DIBON

Naomi sat up. "We weren't there long before he died." She looked at Ruth. "If he had lived, he never would have let his sons marry Moabite women. It is forbidden by our Law. Your gods are an abomination of the God of Israel."

Naomi lay back on her mat. "It doesn't matter now, though. Nothing really matters now."

Ruth said nothing and finally rested on her mat. The stars greeted her in silence, like glimmering guards of the night.

"It is forbidden." The words troubled Ruth, and she tried to escape them by falling asleep. But they followed her to her dreams. Ruth dreamed she was being chased by Elimelech; Elimelech turned into a lion and suddenly Ruth was a deer, running for her life. Then the Old One jumped out from behind a terebrinth tree.

"Come to the altar," she screamed.

Ruth tried to get away, and an eagle flew by. She struggled to keep up with the eagle. *If I could only get to his nest, I'd be safe,* she thought. *I'd be safe.*

NIGHTMARE

She woke up panting for breath. The lion, the eagle, and the Old One disappeared. Naomi slept quietly beside her and the stars still stood guard over the night. For Ruth, sleep would bring no rest.

4

APPROACHING MOUNT NEBO

Before the sun was fully risen, Naomi and Ruth made their way to the northern end of Dibon. In the early morning light, Laban fussed and fumed over the animals, adjusting baskets and wineskins with extreme care. He stood back to survey his handiwork and greeted the two women with a smile.

"A fine morning for travel, don't you think?" he said, pointing to the clear sky with a sweep of his arms. "By the gods of Chemosh and Astarte, may

A FINE MORNING FOR TRAVEL

we have a safe trip."

Naomi rolled her eyes and took her place at the end of the caravan.

"I thought Laban was a Hebrew," Ruth questioned Naomi.

"He is," Naomi replied. "But his faith depends on where he happens to be at the time. In Moab, he appeals to Chemosh for help. In Judah, he prays to the God of Abraham. I suppose if he lived in the Jordan River, he'd pray to the fish."

"Eeyaah!" Laban yelled. The donkeys moved forward and day two of their journey began. Ruth was tired and thoughts of her nightmare from the night before preoccupied her mind. She wondered if the God of Abraham would accept her, now that she had claimed Naomi's God to be her own.

"If all goes well, we will sleep tonight in the shadow of the great mountain of God. Nebo is a day's journey from here." He raised his arms dramatically

NAOMI TELLING OF MOSES.

to the sky. "May the God of Moses watch over us."

Naomi looked at Ruth and smirked.

"Such a man of faith," Naomi said to Laban reverently.

The sturdy merchant blushed with pride and walked slowly back to the head of the troupe.

"Mount Nebo," Naomi explained, "is the mountain Moses climbed to get a glimpse of the land promised to the children of Israel. He was a great prophet of God. But surely Mahlon told you the story."

Ruth shook her head. Mahlon had never shared his faith with her; when she did ask questions, he would change the subject. She supposed now that he felt guilty about his marriage to her.

"The Lord used Moses to lead our people out of the bondage of Egypt into freedom. Moses talked to the Lord face-to-face."

Ruth could hardly believe her ears. "You mean he talked to God? Like you are talking to me?"

"Yes," said Naomi. She looked at her daughter-in-law. "Our God is not a stone image like the gods of your people. He is a living God."

She sighed and fingered her sackcloth. "The Almighty has turned against me. He has forgotten me."

Ruth put her arm around her mother-in-law and tried to comfort her. But her thoughts were of Moses, the man who talked with God. Could such a thing really happen? Could men talk to God? Did He care about His people? Ruth's heart raced with the possibility that these things might be true.

"Did he actually talk with God?" she asked Naomi. "Really?"

Naomi gave her daughter-in-law a stern look. "Of course he did. It is written that God spoke to Moses as a man would speak to his friend. Now don't trouble me with any more questions. You're wearing me out with all this talk."

With that, Naomi walked a little faster and left Ruth to walk alone, wrapped up in her thoughts. Overhead, a caravan of clouds crossed the sky like plumes of white as if to mimic the earthbound caravan that traveled slowly below.

"DID MOSES ACTUALLY TALK TO GOD?"

Hidden from view behind the western hills lay the Salt Sea, and beyond the eastern mountains stretched a mighty desert. Laban skillfully led the donkeys on the narrow trails that led to Mount Nebo. In the afternoon, the mountain loomed into sight and Laban brought the caravan to a halt.

"Rest yourselves for awhile," Laban commanded the weary travelers. "We will arrive at Nebo this evening."

Ruth and Naomi sat down at the side of the road. Naomi handed Ruth a piece of bread and cheese, and they refreshed themselves with water from their water pouch. The afternoon sun lent its gold to the mountains, transforming them with royal luster. Mount Nebo stood like a king in the distance. Ruth turned to ask Naomi another question about Moses, but her mother-in-law had closed her eyes to rest. Instead, she studied a busy harvester ant at her feet, struggling with a bit of cheese.

Laban's familiar yell spurred the group to continue their journey, and several hours later they

"I HAVE SEEN WHAT MOSES SAW."

arrived at the foot of Mount Nebo. They set up camp in the shelter of a small ravine, and one of Laban's servants lit a small fire in the middle of their camp. The sun took back its gold from the mountains and left behind the purple and dark blues of evening.

Everyone gathered around the small fire and had their evening meal. Ruth and Naomi quietly enjoyed dried figs and raisins with their bread. Light from the fire flickered on the travelers' tanned faces.

Laban cleared his throat. "I have been to the highest ridge of this mountain," he said with a flourish. "I have seen what Moses saw when the Almighty showed him the Promised Land." He leaned forward, his face shining in the light and his dark eyes gleaming with excitement.

"When I was a young man," Laban began, "which wasn't so long ago, I might add, I came to—"

"Ayeeee!"

His speech was interrupted by a scream. A black scorpion had darted out from beneath a rock near the fire. Before anyone could move, Laban grabbed his whip and with a stinging slap of leather killed it instantly.

The frightened onlookers stared at Laban with admiration. Even Naomi had to admit it was a spectacular display of skill.

"They only come out at nightfall," Laban explained, putting away his whip. "Now, where was I? Oh yes, I was a young man when I climbed Nebo."

"I made it to the highest ridge, to the top of Pisgah. It was a long and torturous climb," he spoke dramatically, "but I was strong as an ox."

"So what did you see?" one of the servants asked impatiently.

Ruth leaned forward in anticipation.

"What did I see?" Laban repeated the question. "What do you think I saw?"

"Oh, get on with it," Naomi muttered. "Hurry up so we can get some sleep."

Laban frowned at Naomi and continued with his story.

"As God is my witness, I saw what Moses saw.

LABAN'S WHIP

I saw the land of Canaan stretched out like a holy oasis. I saw the valley of the Jordan River, lush and green. I saw the shimmering green of the Salt Sea and the dusty haze of the mountains in the Negeb, where Abraham grazed his sheep. I saw the Sea of Kinnereth and the city Jericho. The mountains of Judea greeted my eyes. I saw it all."

Laban's words danced in the night air, and they swept Ruth away to the top of the mountain. She felt as though her eyes were seeing what Laban saw, what the great prophet Moses beheld when the Lord bade him climb and see the Promised Land. She fell asleep with Laban's words ringing in her ears.

"I SAW IT ALL!"

5

RUTH IS PROTECTED

The next morning, the caravan left the shelter of the great mountain and headed for the plains of Moab. The bright green of the well-watered plains welcomed them in the afternoon sun. As they approached the Jordan River Valley, Laban signaled the group to stop and rest.

"We'll camp here on the plains tonight and tomorrow we cross the river." Laban pointed to the land beyond the river. "The Promised Land," he

CAMP

said with pride. "May the God of Israel bless our journey into His land."

At the back of the caravan Ruth laughed and turned to Naomi. "You were right," she said, chuckling, "Laban's faith changes with the wind!"

"Yes," Naomi replied. "And that is no faith at all."

They set up camp in the late afternoon and, while Naomi rested, Ruth decided to explore the countryside.

"Don't go too far," Laban called after her.

From the top of a small hill, Ruth surveyed the southern end of the Jordan River and watched as it emptied into the Salt Sea. The emerald green of the river valley was a welcome relief to eyes weary of the dusty trail. Tall poplar trees graced the banks of the river, their shiny leaves dazzling like green gems in the sunlight. An occasional breeze stirred the leaves to dance and reveal their soft white undersides.

The mournful sound of a reed pipe called Ruth's attention to a nearby hill. A flock of straggly sheep appeared and spilled over the top of the gentle slope. Their shepherd appeared soon after them, as straggly looking as his sheep. He spotted Ruth on the opposite hill and approached her slowly.

Ruth suddenly felt uneasy; her heart began to pound. She looked around behind her to see if she could spot the camp, but it was hidden from view.

The face of the shepherd darkened as he recognized Ruth's nationality.

He stopped and glared at her. "Moabite scum," he said with disgust. He spat angrily and leaned over to pick up a rock. "Why don't you go back where you came from?"

Ruth froze.

"I would be doing the Almighty One a favor by striking you dead." He raised the rock over his head. Ruth tried to scream, but no sound came out.

"And I would be doing the world a favor by getting rid of you." The crack of a whip pierced the air behind Ruth and she gasped with relief. It was Laban.

LABAN PROTECTING RUTH

The shepherd lowered his rock and smirked at the stout merchant.

"I'm not afraid of you," he spat.

"That's because you're a fool." And with his whip Laban struck the rock out of the man's hand with painful accuracy.

"Now get out of here before I shove your spit down your throat."

Ruth felt her knees give way and the edges of the air grew dark around her. She passed out and Laban grabbed her before she fell to the ground.

She came to as Laban offered her some water.

"It's all right now, he's gone," Laban spoke kindly to her.

Ruth sat up, still trembling with fear.

"Why," she whispered. "Why did he. . ." Her voice faded.

"He was a Hebrew, most likely a son of Gad. They settled in this area after the great exodus." Laban sat down on a large rock next to Ruth. "Before the Israelites crossed the Jordan into the

OFFERING RUTH WATER

Promised Land, they camped here, on the Plains of Moab. And Moabite women tricked some of the soldiers and leaders into worshiping their gods. This brought death into the camp."

Ruth sighed and looked out over the plains. She wondered how life in the Promised Land would be for a Moabite woman.

Laban seemed to read her mind. He looked down at the young widow and spoke quietly to her. "It's not going to be easy for you in Judea," he said. "You saw for yourself how that young fool of a shepherd acted."

Ruth trembled at the thought of what might have happened if Laban had not come along when he did.

"Thank you for helping me," she said. "You probably saved my life."

Laban laughed and shook his head. "Forget it." He stroked his beard. "Perhaps Someone is looking out for you."

He got up and helped Ruth to her feet. "We had better get back to camp."

The setting sun stroked the Jordan River with flames of color before it disappeared behind the distant hills of Judea. Ruth's shadow looked small beside Laban's large one, and she worried over the merchant's words of warning.

Naomi stood at the edge of the camp and greeted Laban and Ruth with a scowl. "Where have you been?" she demanded. She looked at Ruth. "I suppose you were wandering around the countryside, trying to get lost!" She stopped when she saw Ruth's pale face.

"What happened?"

"She almost got herself killed, that's what happened," Laban grunted. "You had better keep a closer watch on her, Naomi."

Naomi glared at the merchant and took Ruth by the hand. "It's time you got some rest, daughter."

After they had eaten, Naomi insisted that Ruth tell her what was wrong. Reluctantly, Ruth told her mother-in-law about the cruel shepherd, and Naomi gasped in horror.

"DON'T TRY TO PROTECT ME."

"But Laban appeared out of nowhere and scared the man away," Ruth said quickly, "so everything is all right now."

Naomi shook her head. "Don't try to protect me, Ruth. You know everything is not all right."

Naomi looked southward toward Moab. "You should have listened to me and stayed with your own people. You would be safe there."

"Would I?" Ruth said, half to herself. She thought of the empty house, Mahlon's tomb, and the screaming of the Old One.

Naomi began to cry. "This never would have happened if you had stayed with your own family."

Ruth put her arms around her. "You are my family now," said Ruth gently. "That is all that matters." She straightened her shoulders and lifted her head with a stubborn look on her face. "I made a promise and nothing is going to stop me from keeping it."

Naomi looked at Ruth and shook her head. "When you get that look, there's no arguing with you!" She gave her daughter-in-law a tired smile

"TOMORROW WE CROSS THE RIVER."

and lay down on her mat. "Try and get some sleep. Tomorrow we cross the river."

Beneath the velvet black sky, the tiny caravan rested. The camp's fire sparkled in the dark plain like a solitary star. Ruth tried to sleep, but the events of the day crowded her mind.

"Hello, old friends," she whispered to the stars. A few of them blinked down at her and Ruth smiled. "Do you know something I don't know?" she asked the night sky.

There was no answer, and Ruth turned and lay on her side. The memory of the shepherd's angry face came to Ruth and frightened her anew, but Laban's words returned to push away the fear.

"Perhaps Someone is looking out for you."

Those words flickered in the darkness of Ruth's sorrow and, for a moment, a tiny spark of faith stirred in the young widow's heart.

"PERHAPS SOMEONE IS LOOKING OUT FOR YOU."

6

CROSSING OVER

"Careful now, or you'll fall off the donkey!" Laban yelled at Naomi as she climbed up on the animal's back.

"Mind your own business!" Naomi yelled back at Laban.

"This is my—"

"I know, I know," Naomi shouted, "this is your business."

Ruth steadied the animal while Naomi settled

NAOMI RIDING A DONKEY

herself on its sturdy back.

"I've ridden donkeys before," she muttered. "I wasn't always poor! Why, Elimelech had several donkeys when we left Bethlehem. But now everything has changed. I have nothing." Her eyes filled with tears. "If only my sons were returning with me to our home."

Ruth stood silently beside the donkey, struggling to hold back her own grief. She rested her hand upon her mother-in-law's arm to comfort Naomi, and the older woman smiled through her tears.

"Dear Ruth!" Naomi sighed and patted her hand. "At least I have you!"

The Jordan River glistened in the morning sun and the poplar trees greeted the travelers with a canopy of green and white. A slight breeze whispered through the branches overhead and suddenly, quietly, it happened again—Ruth thought she heard someone call her name. A strange feeling swept over her, a feeling that this had happened once before. Ruth looked up at the dancing leaves, and then she remembered. It was the day Chilion died. She remembered

RUTH HEARD HER NAME CALLED.

climbing the ridge, grieving for Mahlon.

And there was an eagle, she thought. *I remember I saw an eagle—*

"Eeyaah!" Laban's yell interrupted Ruth's thoughts. "Get ready to cross the River Jordan!"

The donkeys moved forward and Ruth walked beside Naomi's mount. Her heart began to pound as she realized that as she crossed the river, she was crossing over to a new life. She was leaving Moab behind forever.

The water was almost waist deep, and Ruth got soaking wet crossing the Jordan. The smell of salt in the air drew Ruth's gaze southward toward the Salt Sea. Steep sandstone cliffs plunged sharply to the shoreline of the sea.

"That sea is dead, you know," Laban called back to his fellow travelers. "Not a bit of life in it! It's too bitter with salt."

Naomi looked toward the Salt Sea. "My heart feels like that," she said to herself. "Too bitter with sorrow to have any life."

CROSSING THE JORDAN

As the group reached the other side of the river, Laban inspected the caravan and nodded with approval. "We're all here!" he said with satisfaction. "With the blessing of the Almighty, we will travel ten miles today."

Ruth wrung out the water in her clothes as well as she could. Naomi climbed down from the donkey and shook her head at her daughter-in-law.

"I told you to ride one of the donkeys!" she scolded Ruth. "Now look at you!"

"I don't mind," Ruth smiled. "It'll keep me cool."

"Ruth, sometimes I don't understand—"

Naomi was interrupted by Laban's booming voice.

"See that mound over there? Near that grove of palm trees?" Laban pointed toward a clearing in the distance. "That is what used to be the city of Jericho. The city of palms," he said dramatically.

"You know the story of Joshua and Jericho, of course," Laban inquired of Ruth.

Ruth reluctantly shook her head no and Laban

rolled his eyes and sighed.

"Well, I suppose I will have to tell you. Joshua was—"

"Oh, no, you don't," protested Naomi. "It's time we got started. Forget the history lesson. Besides," Naomi said, "we paid for a trip to Bethlehem, not a guided tour of the Promised Land."

Laban stomped off and gave his customary yell to the donkeys. The wilderness of Judea loomed ahead of them, and its barren hills glared down at Laban's troupe. The heat of the sun settled heavily on the travelers, so Ruth's clothes dried quickly.

The trail led upward through the hills, and Ruth urged her mother-in-law to ride on the donkey. When Naomi reluctantly agreed, Ruth grabbed the halter of their donkey and brought it to a stop. After she helped Naomi climb onto the animal, they refreshed themselves with water from their supplies.

Ruth pulled on the halter so they could continue their journey, but to her surprise, the donkey would not budge.

THE DONKEY WOULD NOT BUDGE.

"Oh, no," groaned Ruth. "Laban's going to be so angry!" She watched as the rest of the caravan continued on without them. Ruth pulled harder on the halter and begged the donkey to move, but the animal just gazed at her with mournful brown eyes.

Naomi climbed off the animal, and together the two women urged the donkey to go.

"Forget it," Naomi said as she flopped down by the side of the trail. The caravan had disappeared behind the edge of a hill.

"I'd better run ahead and get Laban," Ruth said.

"And I'll sit here and get ready for a long-winded lecture."

Ruth hurried up the trail; as she reached the bend in the road, she almost ran into someone.

"Now what?" Laban shouted. Ruth stood before him like a forlorn child.

"The donkey won't move. We tried everything but—"

"I turn my back for one minute and you two disappear into thin air!" He marched down the road and Ruth chased after him, apologizing all the way.

Naomi sat by the side of the road, arms folded. Laban came to a halt in front of the donkey and glared at the two women.

"Who stopped the donkey?" he asked. "No one is to stop the donkeys except me. Who stopped the donkey?"

"I did," Ruth said softly, "I was only trying—"

"Never mind!" Laban growled. "Don't you know—"

"Here we go," Naomi said.

"Don't you know it is dangerous to be left alone in the wilderness? There are wild animals in the hills, leopards and bears, not to mention the fierce ones that walk on two legs."

"I'm sorry," Ruth said. "I won't—"

"Furthermore, I am in charge of this trip, and I have never lost a man or animal on the trail. I don't intend to start losing anyone now."

"We know," Naomi replied. "We know. Now, can we go?"

"WHO STOPPED THE DONKEY?"

Ruth helped Naomi get back on the donkey, and Laban walked ahead of them. He looked back at the two women, who smiled cheerfully at him.

"Just don't let it happen again!" He frowned and let out a yell. "Eeyaah!"

The donkey moved immediately and followed his master up the trail. They joined the waiting caravan and continued their journey in the bright afternoon sun. Ruth gazed at the hills and the Judean sky. She caught a glimpse of several gazelles bounding over the high places, their pale brown fur blending in with the color of the hills. On another ridge, wild black goats stood motionless, like a silent cluster of mourners on the barren heights.

As she observed these scenes, Ruth tried to imagine that Mahlon's eyes had seen the same things when he traveled to Moab but thoughts of her husband only renewed her grief, and with every step she took, Ruth wondered if the pain would ever go away.

7

BETHLEHEM!

The night passed quickly in the Judean wilderness. Ruth and Naomi slept in the shelter of a small cave near the camp. When the first rays of morning streaked the sky with light, Laban had everyone up and ready to go.

"It is only ten miles to Bethlehem," he told them. "I expect to make good time and arrive there this afternoon," he continued, "if everyone cooperates." He glared at Ruth and Naomi. "Try and

"TEN MILES TO BETHLEHEM."

keep out of trouble."

Ruth blushed, but Naomi returned his glare. The fresh morning air was bright with the promise of a clear day. The caravan continued its upward climb toward the plateau where Bethlehem was located. The rocky hills crowded the trail like somber spectators watching silently as the little band of people made its way through the wilderness.

Something in the sky caught Ruth's eye and she squinted, trying to get a better look.

Suspended high in the air, barely moving in the sapphire blue sky, several large black birds hovered.

"Vultures." Laban called back in a matter-of-fact voice. "Messengers of death."

Ruth stared up at the scavengers soaring overhead. She shuddered but couldn't take her eyes off them.

"They're probably looking for me," Naomi said. "Unfortunately for them, I'm still breathing."

Ruth looked at her mother-in-law.

"Don't say such things," Ruth scolded her

"I'M SO TIRED."

mother-in-law. "You mustn't talk like that."

Naomi shrugged her shoulders and shifted her sackcloth.

Suddenly, the vultures dropped swiftly to the earth, just beyond a nearby hill. Ruth closed her eyes for a moment and steadied herself against the donkey.

I'm so tired, she thought.

"Feeding time!" Laban yelled. The caravan came to a halt and Laban sauntered to the back of the caravan, inspecting the donkeys as he came.

"We might as well join the vultures and eat now, too." He laughed and slapped his ample sides. "We'll take a short break and be on our way. It won't be long now."

Naomi climbed off the donkey, and the two women sat together by the side of the road and ate their cheese and dried figs.

"This is the last of it," Ruth said, holding up the small, empty basket. She handed her mother-in-law the last piece of cheese. "You'll need your strength for the rest of the journey."

LUNCHTIME

Naomi hesitated, but Ruth had that stubborn look on her face, so she gratefully accepted the cheese. Ruth smiled and gave her mother-in-law a gentle pat on the arm. "Once we get to Bethlehem, we'll be able to get more food."

Naomi's face was etched with worry. "I'm not so sure about that," she said doubtfully.

The heat of the afternoon sun wrapped itself around the little caravan as they made their way to the edge of the wilderness. At times the road looked hazy in the glare, and the air shimmered like liquid light on the road before them. Finally, the travelers left the desolation of the wilderness behind them. The green hills of central Judah filled their eyes, and a cool breeze filtered down from the plateau.

"We're almost there!" Laban shouted back to his weary followers.

Ruth's heartbeat began to race at the thought of approaching Bethlehem. "My new home," she thought.

"It's just beyond this hill," Laban yelled.

"All right, all right, so why don't you announce it to the whole world," Naomi muttered under her breath. She began to tremble as they climbed the sloping hill. "Oh, Elimelech, Elimelech," she whispered. "I've come back to our home with empty arms."

The road widened as they reached the top of the hill. Beyond the fields of ripening grain lay the village of Bethlehem.

"There she is!" shouted Laban. "There she is!"

The sandy-colored mudbrick houses sat close together on the top of a ridge. Here and there, white-washed houses gleamed in the afternoon sun like occasional bright teeth among the faded tan ones. Ruth looked across the fields at Bethlehem and her heart skipped a beat. Her new life was about to begin.

Naomi stifled a sob and stopped in the middle of the road. Ruth quickly put her arms around her mother-in-law.

"I don't think I can bear it," she cried. She clung to Ruth and wept bitterly. "I don't think I can stand to go home alone like this."

"THERE SHE IS!"

"But you're not alone," Ruth implored Naomi. "I'm here. I'll help you."

Naomi smiled sadly at Ruth. "I know, but still—"

Ruth looked down at her dusty feet and spoke softly to her mother-in-law.

"I know I'm not Mahlon or Chilion, but I do love you." Her chin trembled, but she looked Naomi straight in the eye. "I know I can help take care of you."

Naomi wiped the tears from her eyes. She studied her daughter-in-law's face. She wondered to herself where such love came from.

"Let's go," Naomi said finally, "before Laban starts yelling."

Together they caught up with the caravan as they made their way toward the village. Ripened fields of barley and almost-ripened wheat fringed the sides of the road in abundance.

"What did I tell you?" Laban walked back to Naomi and Ruth. "The famine is over! The Almighty has blessed his people with food."

"THE FAMINE IS OVER!"

Naomi nodded in agreement. "It's true. Look at those fields!"

"This is the beginning of the barley harvest," Laban instructed Ruth. "After that, the wheat should be ready."

Ruth listened as Laban gave the detailed history of the harvest.

"And you know, there is provision in the words of the Lord for the poor and the. . .uh. . ." he looked at Ruth, "and the alien." He cleared his throat importantly. "The poor and the alien may glean the field after it is harvested. Crops on the edges of the field are to be left for the poor also."

"What he means, dear Ruth," Naomi snorted, "is that we get the leftovers." Naomi strode past Laban in a huff.

Laban turned to Ruth. "She's a proud woman, Naomi is," he said, "but pride can starve you. My advice to you is to accept the kind provision of the Lord."

Ruth nodded and as Laban walked away, a quiet

"PRIDE CAN STARVE YOU."

peace fell softly on Ruth like a finely woven shawl. "The provision of the Lord," she whispered to herself. She looked toward Bethlehem with new hope ringing in her heart.

8

HOMECOMING

Before the group reached the gate of the village, a flock of little children ran out to greet the caravan. They whooped with excitement when they saw who it was.

"It's Laban!" they shouted. "Laban, Laban, big as a boat! Laban, mean as a goat!" They swooped down on Laban and surrounded him. He laughed and shooed them away.

"Out of my way!" he yelled, waving his arms.

"OUT OF MY WAY OR NO SURPRISES FOR YOU!"

"Out of my way or no surprises for you!" At that, the children respectfully made way for Laban and his donkeys.

Several men and women came out to welcome the travelers. Naomi pulled her sackcloth close and walked toward the gate. She paused for only a moment at the gate where her husband had once sat as an elder of the village. As she continued on, the women stared at her.

"Why, that looks like Naomi," one of them whispered.

"No, that can't be she. She looks so old!"

"Yes, it is too Naomi," one of the older women chimed in. "I ought to know! We were neighbors."

"Naomi!" The woman called after her, and Naomi stopped to face her.

"Hello, Hannah," Naomi said.

"I knew it was you, Naomi."

"Yes, it's I, but don't call me Naomi. Call me Mara, because the Almighty has filled my life with bitterness. I left Bethlehem with my arms full with my

RUTH HEADS FOR NAOMI'S HOUSE.

family, but now the Lord has led me back with empty arms." She turned away and walked through the gate.

"But Naomi—"

"Why should you call me Naomi? Doesn't that mean 'pleasant'? No, Hannah, my name is Mara now."

As Naomi walked away, the villagers crowded around Hannah, thirsting to hear the news. What had happened to Naomi? She was wearing sackcloth! What happened to Elimelech and the two boys?

"I don't know," said Hannah, shaking her head. She watched Naomi's stooped figure trudge slowly toward her old home. "But it looks like she's lost everything."

Ruth waited patiently while Laban untied their few belongings from the donkey's sturdy back. He handed her their mats and baskets.

"Can you carry all that? The house isn't too far."

"I can manage," Ruth replied. "Thank you for your kindness." She smiled. "And your stories."

Laban blushed and grinned at Ruth. "You're welcome, young lady! You're a good listener!" Laban looked around for Naomi. "You'd better catch up with your mother-in-law."

"Yes, I will, and thanks again." Ruth headed in Naomi's direction.

"And Ruth!" Laban called to her and motioned toward the crowd gathered at the gate. "Be careful. Some people's words may be sharper than that shepherd's stone."

Ruth nodded and hurried past the villagers. "Naomi!" she called to her mother-in-law. "Wait for me!"

The women watched as the young woman rushed by.

"Well, who do you suppose that is?" Hannah wondered aloud.

"Why, she's from Moab!" gasped a woman named Judith.

"Maybe she's Naomi's servant," suggested one of the ladies.

"I doubt it," Hannah replied. "By the looks of things, I doubt Naomi would have a servant!"

"SHE'S NAOMI'S DAUGHTER-IN-LAW."

"You don't suppose—"

"Her daughter-in-law!" Judith fairly shrieked. "I say she's Naomi's daughter-in-law!"

All the women began to talk at once. It couldn't possibly be! It wasn't right for a Hebrew to marry an idol worshiper. What a scandal!

Hannah gathered her shawl about her and approached Laban. He was tending his donkeys in front of an admiring audience of children.

"Welcome back, Laban," Hannah said with a friendly voice. "How was your journey?"

Hannah cleared her throat. "Did you make good time?"

"Four nights, five days. The usual." Laban pulled at his black beard. "What is it you really want to know, Hannah?"

The woman didn't hesitate for a moment.

"Who is that young woman with Naomi?"

"Oh, so that's it." Laban spat into the dust. "I figured so much."

"Well, who is she? She looks like a Moabitess."

Laban turned back to his donkeys. "She is," he said tersely.

"Why is she with Naomi?"

Laban struggled with a stubborn knot on one of the halters. Hannah hurried around the donkey and faced the sturdy merchant.

"Well, Laban, who is she?"

"She's Naomi's daughter-in-law!" Laban shouted at Hannah. She jumped back in surprise.

"I knew it!" chortled Judith triumphantly. "I knew it. It's a disgrace," she added, in religious tones.

Laban turned abruptly away from the women, making it clear the subject was closed. "Old hens!" he mumbled under his breath.

While the crowd boiled over with the news, Ruth caught up with Naomi and followed her to their home. It was at the edge of the village, overlooking the terraced fields of grain. Naomi stopped and stared gloomily at her old house. The whitewash had long since faded away, and the door had rotted to pieces. A family of goats had taken up residence inside.

"IT'S A DISGRACE!"

Ruth hurried in and herded the reluctant goats out the door. She quickly swept the clay floor and laid out Naomi's mat so she could rest. Naomi collapsed onto her mat and cried herself to sleep.

The young widow busily finished cleaning the house and setting it in order. She carefully retrieved their only oil lamp from one of the baskets and placed it on the ledge in the wall. Ruth poured some olive oil into the clay lamp and lit it.

The familiar sputtering of the lamp and its warm glow comforted Ruth and made her feel at home. She looked around the room and tried to imagine Mahlon as a young child, running in and out the door. But the room was empty, except for her sleeping mother-in-law, and suddenly Ruth realized once and for all that Mahlon was gone.

She walked through the door and looked out over the fields of grain. In her mind's eye, she looked past the wilderness, past the Salt Sea and into the land of Moab. "Good-bye, Mahlon," she whispered. Ruth let go of him, and peace filled her heart.

"GOOD-BYE, MAHLON."

Evening was drawing near and the fields caught fire with the golden-rose color of the setting sun. Ruth breathed a prayer of new beginnings to the Almighty, and as an evening breeze caressed the ripening grain, Ruth knew in her heart the Lord had not deserted them.

9

RUTH MEETS BOAZ

The next morning, the sharp pangs of hunger wakened Ruth from her sleep. Naomi was already up, standing at the open doorway.

"Good morning, daughter," Naomi said. "How did you sleep your first night in Bethlehem?"

"Very well," Ruth replied. "It's so peaceful here."

"Yes, it is a quiet place." Naomi looked with concern at her young daughter-in-law. "You look a little pale, my dear."

"I'M JUST HUNGRY."

"I'm fine." Ruth rose from her mat and rolled it up. She sat it in the corner next to Naomi's. "I'm just a little hungry, that's all."

Naomi frowned and shook her head. "Just a little? I know better than that, my dear. We haven't eaten since yesterday afternoon." She looked at their empty baskets. "I'm afraid we have no food."

"If you let me, I would like to go to the nearby fields and gather up the leftover grain. Laban said—"

"I know what Laban said," Naomi retorted. Her tone softened and she put her arm around Ruth. "I can't believe it has come to this."

"I'll go at once," Ruth said eagerly. "Perhaps I will find favor with one of the workers and they'll let me glean in their field."

"All right," Naomi agreed. "After all, we really don't have a choice."

Ruth pulled her shawl around her shoulders and hurried out the door. "Be careful!" Naomi called after her.

Naomi stepped outside the door and looked

112

"BE CAREFUL!"

around the familiar neighborhood. Despite all the hardship, she was glad to be home. There were some new houses alongside the old ones, but for the most part nothing had changed.

Nothing except me, she thought. *I used to be so happy, so full of life. And now—*

"Naomi!" A voice called to her from the next house. It was Hannah.

Hannah walked quickly toward Naomi's house and greeted her with a hug.

"Let me get a good look at you," she said kindly. "I didn't get a chance to talk to you yesterday. After all, you'd just come back and you were tired of course, and—"

"Hannah," interrupted Naomi, "would you like to come in and sit down?"

"Of course!" She followed Naomi into the house. They sat down on the flat stones near the empty fire pit that was used for cooking. The lonely oil lamp flickered bravely on its ledge, illuminating the small room.

"IT IS FORBIDDEN."

"Naomi. . ." Hannah hesitated. "Naomi, what happened?"

"Soon after we moved to Moab, Elimelech became ill and died. After his death, the boys married two Moabite women."

"Oh, no!" Hannah's hand flew to her mouth. "I mean, after all, it is forbidden—"

"Orpah and Ruth were very kind to my sons." Naomi's eyes were flashing with anger.

"Mahlon and Chilion did as they pleased after their father died. What was I supposed to do?"

"Now, now, my dear, I didn't come here to get you all upset."

"Then what did you come here for?" Naomi demanded.

Hannah's face reddened. "I just came to see how you were and find out what happened—"

"That's nice," Naomi said sarcastically. "Now be sure everyone in the village gets the news." She pointed to the corners of the almost-empty house. "Don't forget to say we're as poor as beggars."

Naomi's embarrassed neighbor got up quickly and hurried to the door. She paused for a moment and looked at her old friend sitting alone on the floor. "I'm sorry," Hannah whispered. Then she was gone.

Naomi covered her face with her hands and wept bitterly.

The cheerful morning sunlight matched the singing in Ruth's heart as she walked down the road toward the barley fields. Today she would bring home food for her mother-in-law.

"It's in the word of the Lord," she reminded herself. "The foreigners and the widows can pick up the leftovers." She quickened her pace and looked out over the numerous fields of grain. Soon she came upon a barley field where the harvesters had already begun their day's work. Ruth approached the foreman of the workers.

"May I please glean behind the harvesters in your field?"

GETTING PERMISSION TO GLEAN

The foreman eyed Ruth and frowned. "Who are you?"

"I am Naomi's daughter-in-law," she said firmly. "I am from Moab."

The man hesitated and then shrugged his shoulders. "All right," he said. "But stay well behind my workers and don't make any trouble. "I'll be watching you!"

Ruth bowed her thanks and took her place behind the harvesters. The young men were busily cutting through armfuls of barley with their sickles. The women followed behind them, binding the armfuls of grain into neat bundles. Ruth drew open her shawl and began to pick up the leftover stalks.

Occasionally, the workers looked back at the newcomer gleaning behind them. Ruth could hear them talking among themselves, but she worked steadily on, ignoring their stares. The sun shone hotly on the open fields and, after several hours of exhausting work, Ruth rested beneath the workers' shelter.

"Why didn't you stay in Moab, where you

RUTH GLEANING

belong?" The sharp words startled Ruth and she turned to face the accusing voice. It was Judith. "We don't need you and your filthy gods in Judah."

Ruth felt anger boil up inside and threaten to spill out in fierce words, but a calm voice from the other side of the shelter intervened.

"Leave her alone, Judith. The poor girl's got enough troubles without you adding to it." A woman Ruth's age sat down next to her. "My name is Abigail," she said with a smile.

"My name is Ruth," the young widow replied gratefully. "How did you know about me?"

"Laban's my uncle," said Abigail, "and he loves to talk."

Ruth started to laugh, but Judith gave her a harsh look. "I'd better get back to work."

Ruth turned her back on the turmoil in the shelter and returned to her hard labor under the sun. Her heart ached at the thought of Judith's words. She had left the gods of Moab behind in her homeland. Naomi's God was her God now;

couldn't anyone see that?

A strong deep voice interrupted Ruth's thoughts.

"The Lord be with you," he called to the workers.

"The Lord bless you!" They hailed back to him. The man noticed the newcomer in the field and smiled at her. Ruth wondered who the tall man was and watched him as he approached the foreman.

"That's Boaz, the man who owns these fields." Abigail stood at Ruth's side. "He's an important man in Bethlehem."

Boaz joined his foreman and looked out over his fields and workers.

"Seth, how is the harvesting going today?"

"Very well, Boaz. We've had no trouble today."

"Caleb's fields were raided last night. Better keep your eyes open."

"Will do."

The young stranger with auburn hair caught Boaz's attention.

"Who does that young woman belong to, Seth?"

"That's the Moabitess who came back with

BOAZ

Naomi. She asked if she could glean and she's been working hard all day." Seth folded his arms and watched as Ruth continued to gather the fallen grain. "She rested only once in the shelter. Thought she might give us some trouble, but so far—"

"See to it that none of the men trouble her!"

Boaz strode over to the men and gave them clear instructions. Then he approached Ruth and called her to his side.

"Listen, daughter," he said quietly to the young woman. "Stay in my fields to glean. Follow my servant girls and watch where the young men are harvesting. Those are my fields and you may glean as much as you like." He smiled down at Ruth. "I've told my men not to harm you and you can drink from the waterskins as often as you wish."

Ruth stared up into the face of the kind man. His brown hair and beard were speckled here and there with gray, and his warm brown eyes sparkled with life. His face was tan from the sun and, when he smiled, the tiny wrinkles near his eyes smiled too.

HELPING RUTH TO HER FEET

She knelt and bowed before him. "Why do you give me such favor? I am a Moabite. Why should you notice me?"

"I've heard all about you," he said. He took her by the hand and helped her to her feet.

"I know that after your husband died, you came here with your mother-in-law. You've left your home and family to come and live in a land you've never seen before. All because you care about Naomi. May the Lord bless you for what you have done. May you be fully repaid by the Lord, the God of Israel, under whose wings you have found a hiding place!"

Boaz's words ignited Ruth's newborn faith, and it burned brightly in her heart. "You are very kind, sir," Ruth's voice trembled. "Your words bring me great comfort. I hope I can continue to find favor in your sight."

Boaz pulled a stalk of barley and fingered it gently.

"Generally, a farmer gets what he planted. You

"YOU ARE VERY KIND, SIR."

planted seeds of sacrifice and love. And I know you will reap a bountiful harvest."

Boaz looked up at the sun and called out to the workers.

"Time for the midday meal!" He motioned to Ruth to join them and he gave her some roasted grain to eat. He offered her the wine vinegar to dip it in and Ruth's strength was renewed. Boaz gave her so much grain that she put some aside for Naomi.

When Ruth got up again to glean, Boaz gave his men more instructions.

"Let her glean among the sheaves, and pull out stalks for her to gather. And don't give her a hard time about it."

The workers looked at Ruth with new eyes after Boaz arrived. And Judith kept her mouth shut for the rest of the day.

Ruth worked in the field until evening came. Then she threshed the grain and scooped the kernels of barley into her shawl. When she arrived home, Naomi was waiting for her at the door.

THRESHING GRAIN

10

Naomi Forms a Plan

"I was worried sick about you!" Naomi pulled Ruth into the house and sat her down on her mat. "How did everything go?"

Ruth opened her shawl and poured its contents into one of the baskets. Naomi's eyes opened wide as she watched the grain fill the basket to the brim. She looked at her daughter-in-law with amazement.

"Where in the world did you glean today?"

POURING GRAIN INTO A BASKET

Ruth's faced was flushed with color from her hard day's work. She handed Naomi the roasted barley she had left over from the midday meal. "I worked in the fields belonging to a man named Boaz. He was very kind to me."

"I can see that," Naomi said in astonishment. "I can't believe the amount of grain you gathered! May the Lord bless that man for being so good to you!"

Ruth smiled and lay down on the mat. "He told me to glean in his fields for the rest of the harvest."

Naomi's heart was stirred with renewed hope. She looked at the abundant food and at her loving daughter-in-law. "The Lord has not forgotten us," she said. "I can see that His kindness toward us has not stopped."

Ruth nodded with joy at hearing Naomi's words. It was so good to hear happiness in her mother-in-law's voice again.

"Boaz," Naomi said his name thoughtfully. "Why, Boaz is a close relative of my husband! He might be able to help us."

"He told me to stay with his workers," Ruth repeated sleepily.

"That's a good idea, my dear. If you stay with his servant girls, then no one will hurt you."

Naomi's words lulled Ruth to sleep and all was quiet in Bethlehem. Naomi sat up late into the night, watching her tired daughter-in-law sleep. The ever-burning oil lamp cast a glow on the mudbrick walls, and Naomi's heart warmed with the knowledge that God had been with them all along.

The days of the barley harvest passed quickly. Every morning, Ruth walked the dusty road to the fields of Boaz and joined his maidservants there. She worked steadily each day while Naomi took care of the cooking and cleaning. The townspeople kept an eye on the Moabitess and took note of her hard work and devotion to Naomi.

"She can't be all that bad," one of the women whispered as Ruth passed by the well in the center of the village. "She certainly takes good care of Naomi. Poor thing. She must be homesick."

WATCHING RUTH SLEEP

Hannah nodded in agreement. "Poor thing. And I must say, she loves Naomi like she was her own mother!"

"I don't trust her!" grunted Judith. "After all, she's a Moab!" She signaled to the other women to draw closer. "I bet she sneaks off at night and worships that horrible god Chemosh."

The women broke into feverish whispering. Suddenly, the snap of a whip crackled in the morning air and startled the busy group into silence.

"Laban! Why, Laban, son of Jacob, you scared us half to death!" Hannah scolded the portly merchant.

"Oh, I am sorry, ladies." Laban bowed graciously. "I was just practicing. I heard there were vipers near the well that needed tending to."

"Uncle Laban!" Abigail laughed. "You're terrible."

Judith picked up her water jar and stomped off in disgust. The crowd scattered, and Laban sat down near the well.

"So, it worked, didn't it?" Laban slapped his sides and let go of a loud laugh. "There's nothing more

PUTTING TROUBLE TO FLIGHT

satisfying than putting trouble to flight!"

"Honestly, Uncle, you really can be so difficult!"

"Thank you, Abby, my dear. Now shouldn't you be running along to the barley fields?"

"Yes, I'm on my way." She turned to leave.

"Abby—" Laban called his niece to his side. "Ruth works with you, doesn't she?"

"Yes."

Laban lowered his voice. "She's all right, isn't she? None of the men have bothered her, have they?"

Abigail smiled and took her uncle by the hand.

"She's fine. Boaz sees to that! He's warned all the men not to bother her."

Laban sighed with relief. "She's so young and alone, I worry that someone might try—"

"Don't worry, Uncle," Abigail said. "Someone's looking out for her." She looked at Laban with questioning eyes. "If I didn't know better, Laban the independent, tough man, I'd say you care about that young Moabitess."

"Like she was my own daughter," he said quietly.

LABAN'S SECRET IS REVEALED.

"You mean Laban the loner has feelings?" Abigail grinned.

Laban touched his finger to his lips. "Don't tell anyone! It might ruin my image."

Abigail laughed. "Your secret's safe with me!" Laban watched as she hurried down the road toward the fields. The sun was already bright overhead, and it promised to be a sweltering day.

Ruth hummed a song of the harvest as she walked the familiar path to the fields. She paused when she came to a tall pomegranate tree. Among the dark green leaves flashed brilliant red blossoms. Ruth's eyes soaked in the bright colors. Suddenly, a rustle in the nearby bushes caught Ruth's attention. She stiffened with fear. She was too far from the fields to call for help. Memories of the cruel shepherd on the plains of Moab flashed across her mind and paralyzed her with fear.

All at once, someone jumped out at Ruth from

behind the bushes and almost knocked her down. Ruth screamed with fright.

It was a little boy.

Ruth caught her balance, and when she realized how small her attacker was, she laughed with relief.

The child had tumbled to the ground and was trying to get up and run.

"Hey!" Ruth reached for his chubby little hand and helped him to his feet.

The little boy's dark hair was a tangle of curls. He pushed the curls out of his eyes and looked up at Ruth.

"My grandma says that all Moabite women 'tice men of Israel to their doom. Are you going to 'tice me to my doom?" He made himself as tall as possible. "I'm a man, you know." His little chin quivered.

Ruth stifled a laugh. "I think the word is *entice*, and, no, I am not going to entice you to your doom. You don't have to be afraid of me. You look like a very brave boy. What's your name?"

"Gideon."

"Where are you going in such a hurry?"

ATTACK!

"Laban the merchant promised me a ride on one of his donkeys. He'll prob'ly put me on the meanest one 'cause I'm so brave."

Ruth nodded in agreement. "You better run along then, Brave Gideon."

Gideon grinned with satisfaction and hurried off to high adventure.

Ruth gazed with longing at the little figure running toward Bethlehem. In ten years of marriage to Mahlon, she had never been blessed with a baby. Her heart ached for a moment, but the bright sun reminded her there was work to do.

Every day, Boaz came to the fields to check on the workers, and every day he greeted Ruth with a smile. His kindness made her feel at home in Bethlehem.

After a vigorous day's work, Ruth enjoyed climbing the outside stairs to the roof of their home. After enduring the heat of the fields, Ruth reveled in the cool caress of the evening breezes. One evening, Naomi joined her daughter-in-law on the roof. Ruth noticed

JOINING RUTH ON THE ROOF

that Naomi had an "I have a plan" look on her face.

"What's on your mind, Mother?" Ruth asked.

Naomi cleared her throat and looked lovingly at her daughter-in-law.

"Ruth, you have been so good to me. You have treated me as if I were your own mother. Now I want to do something for you."

Ruth protested, but Naomi continued.

"After all you have done for me, shouldn't I try to find a home for you, a home where you would be taken care of?" Naomi leaned forward earnestly. "In Israel, there is a special provision for the widow. If your husband dies and leaves no son to inherit his property, then a brother or close relative must marry the widow. The first son would be considered the dead husband's son, so his name and property would not be lost in Israel. And isn't Boaz our relative? That makes him a kinsman-redeemer."

"Boaz?" Thoughts of Boaz's strength and kindness filled Ruth's mind.

"Listen carefully, my dear. The barley harvest is

A FINAL HUG

almost over. Tonight Boaz will be winnowing barley at the threshing floor. Wash yourself and put on your perfume and your best clothes.

"Go down to the threshing floor and wait until Boaz is finished with the harvest meal. Don't let him see you. Then watch to see where he goes to sleep. Then go to him, uncover his feet, and lie down there. When he awakes, he will tell you what to do."

Ruth looked at her mother-in-law in amazement. Naomi's eyes were filled with love. "Trust me, daughter."

Naomi reached over and hugged Ruth tightly. "Hurry now and get ready."

Inside the house, Ruth retrieved her long white tunic and her blue shawl from one of the baskets stacked in the corner of the room. She was ready in no time and, with a final hug from her mother-in-law, Ruth left for the threshing floor. Naomi watched until Ruth disappeared down the road, her soft blue and white clothes blending with the tender blue haze of evening.

11

AT THE THRESHING FLOOR

At the threshing floor, Boaz and his men winnowed the barley. With large wooden forks, they flung the beaten grain into the air. The evening breezes carried away the light straw and dust, while the heavier kernels of barley fell to the floor. While they worked, their talk and laughter filled the air. It was a bountiful harvest, and the wheat fields promised to be bountiful as well.

Ruth drew near to the threshing floor and hid

BOAZ WINNOWING

herself in the shadows of a myrtle tree.

"Boaz," a young boy called shyly to the man. "Tell us about the time some nomads attacked in the wheat fields and you ran them off all the way to the wilderness."

Boaz laughed and with strong arms pitched the grain into the air. "You've heard that story a thousand times!"

"Please," several young voices chimed in. "Tell us again!"

"All right, all right," said Boaz. "I can see I have no choice!"

Light from the torches lit up the large round threshing floor and the edges of the nearby fields. The eager faces of the youths shone in the flickering light, their eyes sparkling with expectation. Boaz noticed a little child among the group.

"Why, Gideon! What are you doing out here tonight?"

"My mother said I could watch the winning if Micah watched me!" He looked up at his older brother with a pleading look.

"It's winnowing, *not* winning, and if you don't keep quiet I'll take you home right now!" Micah said impatiently.

"Okay, boys, let's not fight." Boaz smiled down at Gideon. "This story may be scary for you, young fellow."

"I'm Brave Gideon," the little soldier said proudly.

"Yeah, right," Micah whispered sarcastically. Gideon stuck out his tongue and turned his attention to Boaz.

"Several years ago, just before the wheat harvest, the Philistines had been raiding the fields of the neighboring villages. We knew it was only a matter of time before they came to Bethlehem."

The young boys' eyes grew wide. Gideon hid behind his brother.

"As you know, our village is small and we didn't have enough men to fight them off man for man, so we devised a plan."

"A plan?" Gideon whispered from behind Micah.

BOAZ TELLING AN ADVENTURE STORY

"Hush up." Micah frowned at his little brother.

"The raids were always carried out at night, when everyone was asleep. So Seth and I and a handful of men would keep watch every night. One night, our guard duty paid off. We discovered a band of the thieves in the middle of one of my fields." Boaz paused and looked up at the moon. "There was no moon that night, so it was hard to see."

"You mean it was dark?" Gideon asked.

"It was *very* dark," Seth said in a serious tone. The foreman hefted a shovelful of grain into the air. "Tell him what happened next, Boaz."

Boaz nodded and gave Gideon a wink.

"The Philistines had stationed their watchman at the edge of the field. Fortunately for us, he had fallen asleep. We stole his weapons, and in the cover of the night, with only the stars shining above, we quickly lit the torches we had set up all around the field. We caught the thieves by surprise."

Seth continued. "Boaz yelled out, 'We've got you surrounded. If you don't get out, we'll set this field on fire and burn you alive!' The only thing those marauders could see were the torches. Well, they ran out of there as fast as they could, and Boaz chased them with their own spears toward the wilderness. And for all we know, they're still running!"

Boaz laughed and raked the grain into a pile. "We're almost finished here. Why don't you boys get something to eat?"

Boaz and the men finished the winnowing and joined the others and sat down at the harvest feast. The joy of a bountiful harvest shone on the faces of the people, and their laughter danced in the night air. The torches joined the dance, gleaming and flickering in the breeze.

Ruth waited patiently in the shadows. Finally the feast was over and most of the people returned to their homes. Boaz and a few workers remained at the threshing floor to guard the grain.

"It's been a good day's work," Boaz said to his men. "May the Lord bless you."

"The Lord bless you!" they answered.

BOAZ SMELLS A TRACE OF PERFUME.

Boaz lay down by the pile of grain and covered himself with his cloak. His heart was warm with happiness of the day, and he took a deep breath of the evening air.

Boaz sat up for a moment. There was a trace of perfume in the air.

That's funny, Boaz thought. *That smells like some kind of perfume.* He shook his head and laughed to himself. *I must be extra tired!*

Ruth waited until everyone was asleep. Then she softly walked over to Boaz. She was afraid the pounding of her heart would waken him. Carefully, she uncovered Boaz's feet and lay down. The flames of the torches had dwindled and Ruth looked up at the midnight sky. The stars greeted her with their customary sparkle and Ruth smiled, remembering her long journey from Moab.

"And look where the journey has brought me," she whispered to herself. "Oh, Lord, please be with me now." She began to tremble. What if Boaz didn't want her? After all, she was a foreigner! "No," she

RUTH LYING AT THE FEET OF BOAZ

said to herself. "I won't be afraid. The Living God will watch out for me."

In the deepest chamber of the night, the bark of a fox echoed in the hills and Boaz woke with a start. The gentle scent of perfume hung in the air like a fragrant messenger. Boaz turned over, and to his surprise there was someone lying at his feet.

"Who are you?" he whispered.

Ruth sat up.

"I am Ruth, your maidservant. Spread your cloak of protection over me, for you are a kinsman-redeemer."

Joy swept through Boaz's heart like a rushing wind.

"May the Lord give you happiness, young lady, because this loving kindness you show tonight is even greater than the love you showed before in coming to Bethlehem. Instead of going after any of the younger men, rich or poor, you have chosen to come to me."

Ruth shivered in the moonlight.

"Now, don't be afraid, young lady. I will do all that you need for me to do. Surely all of Bethlehem knows what a woman of strength you are!"

Boaz continued in a whisper, while the other men dreamed of Philistine raids and harvest feasts.

"It's true that I am a near kinsman, but there is a man who is a closer relative than I am. Stay here tonight, and in the morning, if he will accept the role of kinsman-redeemer, very well, let him do so. But if he does not, I promise, as surely as the Lord lives, I will be your kinsman-redeemer. Stay here until the morning comes."

Ruth lay back at Boaz's feet. He gently covered her with his cloak. She wondered who the other relative was and what he was like. What if that man decided to redeem her? But Boaz was so strong and kind, surely the other man wouldn't— "Stop it," Ruth said to herself. She pulled her thoughts back to the truth that was now written on her heart—the living Lord would watch over her.

Boaz lay quietly looking at the moon while his

"SHE CAME TO ME!"

heart pounded with joy. *I can't believe she came to me!* he thought. *She came to me! She's so beautiful and kind!. What if that man agrees to redeem Ruth?* He looked up at the night sky, mindful of the woman at his feet. *The Lord's hand is in this,* he thought. *The Lord has a plan. He will lead the way.*

His thoughts became peaceful and the hours passed quickly. Early in the morning before the sun rose, Ruth got up quietly to leave. Boaz nodded his approval.

"It's good that you go now, while it is still dark." He looked at his sleeping workers. "We don't need ugly rumors flying through Bethlehem. Now bring you shawl over here and hold it out for me."

Ruth took off her shawl, and as she held it, Boaz filled it with six measures of barley.

Boaz placed the grain-filled shawl over Ruth's shoulders and smiled down at her. "I don't want you to return to your mother-in-law with empty hands."

"Thank you," she whispered.

Ruth left the threshing floor and returned home.

NAOMI HEADING FOR THE VILLAGE GATE

Naomi fluttered around her, with questions flying. "So what happened, daughter? How did it go?"

She helped Ruth with her shawl and together they put the grain into one of the baskets. Ruth told Naomi everything that had happened. She held up the basket of grain.

"He sent this to you," she said with a smile.

Joyfully, Naomi clasped her hands together and motioned for Ruth to sit down.

"Stay here until you know how everything turns out." Naomi put on her own shawl and went to the door. "Boaz will not rest until he settles the matter today."

Naomi left the house and headed for the place where all legal business took place: the gate of the village.

12

BOAZ CHOOSES RUTH

The gate of the village was already open and bustling with activity. Women were gathered at the well to draw water for the day; the nearby marketplace was open for business.

Boaz went to the gate and sat down to wait. He watched as people traveled in and out of the gate. They greeted him as they passed through, and Boaz smiled in return, barely noticing his friends and neighbors. But he kept watching the crowds carefully.

BOAZ WAITING AT THE GATE

Hannah greeted Abigail at the well and put down her clay jug.

"Well, it's a busy morning in Bethlehem," she said brightly.

"It certainly is," responded Abigail. "Look, there's Boaz, sitting at the gate. I wonder what he's doing?"

"So it is! Maybe he's going to bring something up before the elders. There have been a few more raids in the last few weeks," said Hannah thoughtfully. "Maybe it's about that."

"I'd say he's looking for someone," Judith piped.

Hannah looked at Judith. "How can you tell?"

"Just look at him!" Judith said. "He's watching those crowds like an eagle searching for prey. I say he's looking for someone!"

"You're right," agreed Abigail. "I wonder who—"

"Hush now," interrupted Hannah. "Here comes Laban."

"Good morning, ladies." He smiled broadly. "How is everything at the well today? Is there still water in the well of Bethlehem? And who is it you

165

WOMEN AT THE WELL

are staring at?"

He followed their gaze to the gate.

"So it's Boaz you're concerned with today. Shall I go and tell him you're watching out for him? I'm sure it would put his mind at ease!"

"Oh, Uncle Laban." Abigail sighed.

"Why don't you mind your own business?" snorted Judith.

Laban laughed out loud and headed for the marketplace.

"I've got some fine pottery from Moab for sale, ladies," he called to them. "And lamb's wool, too!"

Finally, Boaz spotted the man he was looking for. He called out to him. "Ethan! Come here and sit down at the gate."

The man came over and sat down next to Boaz. "What is it, Boaz?"

"I have some business to conduct with you. Will you wait here while I gather the ten elders of the village?"

"I will wait," he said.

BOAZ GIVING ETHAN THE PROPOSITION

Boaz left and called together the ten elders of Bethlehem and asked them to assemble at the gate. Soon a curious crowd gathered near the gate.

"What do you suppose—?" Hannah whispered to Abigail. "Look! There's Naomi! What's she doing here?"

"Be quiet!" Judith hissed. "I can't hear a thing."

Boaz sat down next to the man named Ethan. All eyes were on Boaz as he began to speak. The morning sun glittered above the scene, and all was quiet except for the occasional braying of a donkey and the crying of a baby lamb.

"Thank you all for being here," Boaz began. He nodded to the elders and turned toward Ethan.

"As you know, Naomi has returned from Moab under difficult circumstances. Because of this, she is going to sell the property that belonged to her husband, Elimelech."

"Just as I thought!" whispered Judith.

"Shh!" Hannah leaned forward to get a better look.

"I wanted to let you know about this, so that you can buy it with these people and the elders as witnesses. If you want to buy it, then do so. You are the next of kin to Elimelech, the land is rightfully yours. However, if you do not want to redeem this property, let me know now. After you, I am the closest relative."

Naomi's heart pounded as she waited to hear the man's reply. The crowd strained with excitement. Laban watched with concern in his eyes.

The man's eyes lit up at the thought of adding more property to his own. He stroked his beard and stood to his feet.

"I will redeem it."

The crowd burst into a torrent of chatter. Laban spat into the dust, but Naomi kept her eyes on Boaz.

"Very well," replied Boaz firmly. He stood to his feet beside Ethan. His tall, strong frame towered over his relative. "But when you redeem the property of Naomi and Ruth the Moabitess, you must marry the wife of the deceased and give her a son. It is the duty of a kinsman to keep the name of the dead alive along with his inheritance."

Ethan's face darkened with worry. "Ruth the Moabitess! If I marry her, that would ruin my own inheritance! You redeem it yourself. I just can't." Ethan pulled off his sandal and held it out to Boaz.

In those days in Israel, a business deal was made legal by the seller giving the buyer his sandal. Ethan was offering Boaz the right to redeem Naomi and Ruth's property.

Boaz bowed graciously and took the sandal. He turned to face the elders seated at the gate and the crowd assembled there and held the sandal up in the air.

"On this day, you are witnesses that I have purchased all the property of Elimelech, and all that belonged to Chilion and Mahlon." His voice filled the air. "You are also witnesses that I have chosen Ruth the Moabitess to be my wife, in order to keep the name of Mahlon alive along with his inheritance. His name will not be cut off from among his family, nor from the place of his nativity."

The crowd boiled over with joy. The elders stood and nodded their approval. "We are witnesses," they said. Everyone began shouting all at once. "We are witnesses!"

One of the elders lifted his hands to heaven. "May the Lord cause the woman coming into your house to be like Rachel and Leah, who built the house of our father Israel. May you be great and prosper in the land of Ephrathah, and may you become famous in Bethlehem."

"May the lord make your house like the house of Perez, the son of Tamar and the royal line of Judah, because of the children of the Lord will give you through this young woman."

"Amen!" everyone shouted.

Naomi wept for joy, and the women surrounded her with cries of happiness. There was a steady flow of congratulations, and plans were quickly made for a feast to celebrate the new marriage. In the midst of all the happy commotion, Boaz slipped away from the crowd.

WEEPING FOR JOY

13

A Time of Celebration

Ruth sat alone in the little house, wondering what was happening down at the village gate. The faithful oil lamp sputtered and glowed, and Ruth watched the flame cast its light against the wall.

She marveled at the events of the last few days, and her heart beat faster when she thought of the night before. What would happen today? Who would come and get her? Who would be her kinsman-redeemer?

"YOU ARE MY WIFE NOW."

"Ruth!" Startled by the sound of a voice at the door, the young woman turned around to see Boaz standing in the doorway. It was the first time he had ever called her by name.

The man's voice danced in the air and struck a chord of remembrance in Ruth's heart. It was as if she had heard his voice a long time ago, before she ever knew him. Ruth closed her eyes and listened.

As Boaz called out her name again, suddenly Ruth understood. The Lord, the Living Lord knew her name! He loved her and would always take care of her. She had come to trust under the Lord's wings, Boaz had said. Now she knew God had given her Boaz! But beyond the tender care of those she could see and touch, Ruth saw the Living God. She knew she would never be alone again, no matter what the future held for her.

Ruth was speechless. Boaz walked over and gently took her by the hand.

"It's all right," he said. "You are my wife now."

The young widow looked up and saw the love in

Boaz's heart shining through his eyes. She let the joy of the moment wash over her in waves of comfort.

"Thank you," she finally spoke, softly.

Boaz put his arms around Ruth. "And don't worry about Naomi. She'll live with us." He smiled down at her. "Let's go home."

The sound of laughter and excited voices filled the air as Naomi and her friends approached her house. Boaz and Ruth greeted them at the door and Naomi enveloped Ruth in a warm hug.

"I am so happy for you!" Naomi cried. "The Lord has not forgotten us!" She looked up at Boaz with deep respect in her eyes. "And thanks to you, the names of my husband and my sons will not be lost in Israel." Naomi bowed to the ground before Ruth's kinsman-redeemer.

Boaz shook his head and helped Naomi to her feet.

"It is my privilege," he said. "Not another word about it. Now let's go! I imagine the celebration has already begun!"

"You run along," Naomi urged the couple. "I have something I have to do first."

Boaz and Ruth left Naomi in the house and her friends joined them. Naomi looked around the small house that had been her home. Memories of Mahlon and Chilion chasing each other around the room crowded her thoughts and she smiled. She could hear Elimelech scolding them and laughing at their antics.

Naomi gathered the happy memories from every corner of the room, but decided to leave the sorrow behind. She found the basket she was looking for and changed her clothes.

When she arrived at the celebration, Ruth noticed the change immediately.

"Mother!" she exclaimed. "Your sackcloth!"

"It's gone," replied Naomi.

"You look wonderful!"

Boaz's home was overflowing with guests. Boaz's servants busily prepared the food and wine for the midday feast. It seemed like all of Bethlehem was coming to take part in the celebration.

WEDDING CELEBRATION

Ruth was overwhelmed with all the attention, so she retreated to the roof of Boaz's home. She looked down at the courtyard below and watched as more people joined the party. The sun was brilliant and hot, but Ruth preferred to stay on the roof.

The wheat fields surrounding Bethlehem swayed like golden ripples in the breeze, and the terraced hills boasted an abundance of olive and grape vineyards. Beyond the vineyards and fields of grain, flocks of sheep and goats speckled the land with black and white.

"It's a beautiful place, isn't it?" A familiar voice spoke.

Ruth twirled around. "Laban!"

"I am so proud of you," the merchant said with a smile.

Ruth laughed. "Thank you! I'm glad you're here, Laban. I wanted to thank you again for all your help, and especially for saving my life. How could I ever repay you?"

"Forget it," Laban said.

LABAN TELLS ANOTHER STORY.

"Oh, I'll never forget it. And I told Boaz all about it."

"You didn't have to do that," Laban protested.

Ruth stubbornly shook her head. "We'll never forget it."

Laban laughed. "I know when I'm beaten!"

The two stood together silently for a few moments, surveying the lovely landscape. The hills of Judea rolled faithfully to the horizon in shades of green and blue. Laban turned his eyes eastward and then looked at Ruth.

"I know a way you can repay me," he said.

"Wonderful!" Ruth replied eagerly. "What can I do for you?"

"Listen to me tell you one more story."

Ruth clapped her hands together. "Of course! I'd love to hear another story." She sat down and motioned for Laban to do the same. The merchant bowed to the young lady and took a seat beside her.

Laban pointed toward the east. "Beyond the wilderness of Judea, as you know, lies the Jordan River

Valley. You remember what I told you about Moses?"

Ruth nodded eagerly. "He led the people out of Egypt and climbed the mountain to speak with the Lord."

"Yes, yes, that's right!" said Laban. "And it was the Plains of Moab that the people camped before entering the Promised Land."

The poplar trees and the smell of the Salt Sea paraded before Ruth's mind.

"They crossed over to Jericho, right?"

"Yes, that's right. Now Moses died, and a brave man named Joshua became the leader. He planned to conquer Jericho, but first he sent spies to the city. Those two spies went to the house of a Canaanite prostitute named Rahab to get information."

"Did she help them?" Ruth interrupted.

"She certainly did!" Laban replied.

"When the king of Jericho heard there were spies in the city, he sent a search party to look for them. Rahab hid them on the roof of her home."

"Why did she do that? Then what happened?"

RAHAB HID THE SPIES.

"Will you let me tell the story?" Laban rolled his eyes in exasperation.

"I won't say another word."

"All right then. Now, where was I? Oh, yes, Rahab hid the spies on the roof of her home. After the king's men left, Rahab went up to the roof and told the men she had heard how their God had delivered the Israelites out of Egypt and defeated all their enemies on the way. She told them she knew their God was the God of heaven and earth, and she asked that she and her family be spared when the Israelites attacked Jericho."

"Did they—" Ruth covered her mouth with her hand as Laban scowled.

"The spies agreed to show her mercy and instructed her to tie a scarlet cord in the window of her home. They told her to have all her family in her house and to stay there until the fighting was over. No one would attack the house with the scarlet cord."

"The Lord told Joshua to have the people march around Jericho six days. On the seventh day, they blew on their trumpets and let out a shout. The walls of Jericho fell to the ground in a roar of rubble."

Ruth's eyes were wide with wonder but she didn't say a word.

"The Lord gave them the victory, and Jericho was completely destroyed." Laban paused. "Everything, except for Rahab's family."

"Rahab lived with the Israelites for the rest of her life. An Israelite named Salmon married her, and they had a son. In fact, she just died a few years ago."

"A few years ago!" Ruth blurted out. "Did you know her, Laban?"

Laban nodded. "The name of her son is Boaz."

The impact of Laban's words resounded in Ruth's heart. She was stunned.

"You mean Boaz's mother was. . .a Canaanite?"

"Yes, she was. Rahab embraced the faith of the Israelites when she heard of the power of their God. Her life was spared because of the kindness she showed to the spies when she hid them from the king."

Ruth's eyes filled with tears. "What a merciful, wonderful God! It had to be the Lord who led me to the fields of Boaz, to a man who would look beyond my nationality and see my heart. Oh, Laban," Ruth said, weeping, "thank you so much for telling me!"

Laban turned away so Ruth would not see his tears. "It's all right," he mumbled.

Laban stood to his feet. "I have to go now, I'm leaving early tomorrow for Joppa. I've got some business there to take care of."

Ruth wiped her tears and gave Laban a hug. "Thank you for everything."

They heard the sound of hurried steps on the stairway. It was Boaz.

"There you are!" he said warmly. "I've been looking all over for you. It's time for the feast and everyone is waiting for the bride!"

Ruth blushed at the word *bride*. "I'm so happy I can hardly breathe!"

"Ruth!" Naomi's voice called up from the courtyard.

"Coming!" she called back. "Good-bye, Laban. I hope we see you again soon." With that, the young woman hurried down the stairs to her mother-in-law.

Boaz placed his hand on Laban's shoulder. "I want to thank you for all you've done for Ruth. She told me how you saved her life.

"I will always be grateful to you. If you ever need my help, just let me know."

"Thank you, Boaz, but you know me! I don't need anyone's help!" He laughed and slapped his friend on the back.

"Congratulations on your new wife." He lowered his voice. "Take good care of her, Boaz. She's like a daughter to me."

"You know I will! Now, come join the feast!"

The feast lasted the whole day and well into the night. The next day, it was a happy memory, and one year later another celebration was held—Ruth gave birth to a baby boy.

The women of the neighborhood named him Obed, which means "servant."

RUTH'S SON

"Praise be to the Lord," Hannah exclaimed to Naomi. "The Lord has given you a kinsman-redeemer! May this child be famous in Israel! He will restore your life and care for you when you are old." She looked at Ruth. "For your daughter-in-law, who loves you dearly and is better to you than seven sons, has given birth to him."

Naomi took the baby and held it in her arms.

"I never thought I'd have a grandson! Blessed be the Lord!"

Boaz's home resounded with the happy sounds of celebration in honor of Ruth's first-born son.

The autumn rain was falling steadily now and the reds and yellows of the poppies blurred together in the downpour.

A strong voice called to the young woman.

"Ruth! You're getting drenched." Boaz wrapped his cloak around her and they walked back to the house together. The rain showered the land with refreshment and mingled with Ruth's gentle tears of joy.

She was home.

EPILOGUE

When Obed, the son of Boaz and Ruth, grew up, he had a son named Jesse. When Jesse grew up, he had a boy who one day killed a giant by the name of Goliath. He killed him with a stone from his slingshot. That boy later became king of Israel. His name was David.

Many generations later another boy was born in Bethlehem, descended from David, descended from Obed. His name was Jesus.

YOUNG READER'S CHRISTIAN LIBRARY

Be sure to check out other books in this series!

Written just for readers
ages 8 to 12, these stories
really come to life with
dozens of illustrations. Kids
will learn about the people,
events, and ideas that had a
tremendous impact on
Christian history.

Paperback, 192 pages each

ONLY
$1.49 EACH!

Elijah
Jesus
Abraham Lincoln
Samuel Morris
Paul
Ruth

Esther
Eric Liddell
Lydia
Florence Nightingale
The Pilgrim's Progress
Sojourner Truth

Available wherever Christian books are sold.